SHADOW CROSSING

SHADOW CROSSING

Lea Harper

Black Moss Press
2000

© Copyright Lea Harper 2000

Published by Black Moss Press at 2450 Byng Road, Windsor, Ontario, N8W 3E8. Canada. Black Moss books are distributed in Canada and the U.S. by Firefly Books. All orders should be directed there.

Black Moss would like to acknowledge the Canada Council for the Arts for its publishing program. Thanks also to the Ontario Arts Council for its financial assistance this year.

CATALOGUING IN PUBLICATION DATA

Harper, Lea
    Shadow Crossing

Poems.
ISBN 0-88753-346-9

1. Aging — Poetry. 1. Title.

PS8565.A6422S53 2000   C811'.54   C00-900876-4
PR9199.3.H34582S53 2000

Acknowledgements

Some of these poems, in these or earlier versions appeared or will appear in: *Canadian Dimension*, *The Canadian Forum*, *CV2*, *Descant*, *Event*, *Grain* and *People's Poetry Letter*; and in the following anthologies: *I Want To Be The Poet Of Your Kneecaps* (Black Moss Press), *Water*, The Beehive Press, UK.
"The Colours of Love" was awarded the 1999 LaPointe Prize. "Battle of The Pines" and "A Far Cry" won People's Political Poem contest, 1998.

For thoughtful criticism, the author thanks Betsy Struthers, Florence Treadwell and Marty Gervais along with Jane Bow, Mary Breen, Troon Harrison, Julie Johnston, Patricia Stone, Christl Verduyn and Allan Briesmaster for continual support and encouragement. For financial assistance in the writing of this book, the author thanks the Canada Council and theOntario Arts Council.

Cover design by John Doherty. Cover photograph by Marty Gervais.

For Larry Everitt

CONTENTS

THE PATH OF NO RETURN

In Apogee   11
It's How You Work Out the Evil   12
Other Wars   13
The Circuitous Path   15
The Golden State   19
Gone to the Dogs   21
Independence Day   23
In Your Wake   25
Atonement   26
The Basket   27
I Have The Power   30
Shadowcrossing   31

BLOOD OF THE EARTH

The Next Move   35
Battle of The Pines   36
Crossover   38
What Would You Do Anyway?   40
Dreamers Rock   41
Post War   43
The Moon Had A Sister   45
Blackthorn Winter   47
What the Thunder Brings   48
Accidents   50
The Lake Thereafter   53
The Ghost of God   55
The Book of Weeds   57

TRUE COLOURS

Rota   63
The Colours of Love   65
True Colours   66
Butterfly Picking   67

Day of the First Mother   69
The Call   71
A Far Cry   73
The Lake in July   76

THE PATH OF NO RETURN

In Apogee

Without a sundial for the shifting zodiac
we are accidents of chance
sightless to circumstance
strangers in apogee

Longing binds us to this world -
a glittering ghost dance
an undelivered pearl

And mated to the earth like preying mantis
it is emptiness that topples us
like hollow trees taken by wind

The long years, finally to face love

Today, I look out the picture window
at the flashing lake
and marvel at the things we cannot touch
In the shadow of Shiva's arms
hummingbirds levitate above the fuschia
like little yogis

A barge drifts past
Everyone I know is on it
There is nothing more they can tell me

The waves drink the waves

It's How You Work Out The Evil

You are no longer the boy from Manitoulin
with the sun-dappled hair
bareback on his grandfather's horse
the kid the cousins despised
for more than his light skin
Having nothing themselves to ride
they drove you into the ground
made you crawl home
bleeding from the knees and ass
tongue tied with shame

You are no longer the frightened boy
your grandfather carried to a secret place
where the copperhead slid out of the bush
into the circle he'd made with kerosene
saying only of the attack:
They are like the serpent who has no spine

Your assailants have forgotten you
But when their firstborn
wobbled like soft-boiled eggs
their bones unfused
you saw the circle come around
and your grandfather step inside
the wind warbling in his throat
face of a warrior streaked with char

An island is a circle without corners to hide
Freedom - a canvas of walled cities
you sketch yourself into
the pentimento of a life
painted over and over
with the muscled limbs of stallions
and ghost riders -
a spur of wind, a hint of hooves
a blur of dust and light

Other Wars

When rage exceeds love...

Heart failure, they said as they carried you out
but the heart had failed long before this

Climbing a ladder to remove the storms
you broke a window
then beat the shutters with a rake
It took twelve beers to hold you down
your supper in the sink, your wife sent to bed

After harder drinks
you show us with swizzle sticks
how you flew over Tangiers
Whoosh, whoosh
The olives drop like bombs
With a napkin and toothpick
you parachute into the couch
snoring like thunder

Your heart quit at 1:00 A.M.
when I awoke to the presence -
symbols forming on the wall
From the apex of a hooded star
two eyes like embers
then a cross - two lines of blood

The space you once inhabited
buzzes like a burnt power line -
a high pitched tension in my head

By day, a relief to be rid of you
by night, a torment of recurring dreams:
    On hands and knees
    I crawl toward your room
    clawing my face and arms

Inch by inch
bearing my crosses of ill will

It's taking forever to get there
and when I do it will be time to leave

The Circuitous Path

1986   1968

I know where I am...
               I never knew where they were taking me...

an abandoned building on the waterfront
midnight, answering a film call —
segment of Night Heat

                Ward 3. Removed from the world
                for therapy: loading balloons
                into plastic bags for 75 cents

Wardrobe lady dresses me
from a bin marked sleazewear
I will be shot outside —
a hooker in February

                I won't change out of my dress
                The wooden beads and ankh
                are my protection

Between takes, a raft of extras
warming our hands on cups of coffee
popping donuts like amphetamines
400 toxins, 40 chemicals in Lake Ontario
A foul wind cuts us to the bone

                We eat in silence, with fingers or spoons —
                cornpaste and custard
                Fights break out. My dose increases
                Tongue so thick I lose the power of speech

3 am:
The thin girl beside me
who has hardly spoken
is treated for hypothermia

        They stand over me while I bathe
        I'm handed soap, a razor
        without a blade

Inside:
latrine-green walls
faint smell of disinfectant
dust trapped in the nostrils

        A prison during W. W. II —
        lake barely visible through the bars
        The scent of lilacs is all I have

Trying not to trip
over the black cables duct-taped to the floor
Or listen to the talk:
Director's edgy, crew complain of headaches
Some location! A nut house full of haunting
Can you hear that? A floor above us
the terminally insande died. All boarded up now

        Underground tunnels, secret examinations
        Tanya escapes with the breadman
        Sylvie found dead by the water
        The nightpills take hold
        somewhere between first and second floor
        Voided, we collapse on row beds
        dream nothing

Must be mourning doves, pigeons in the rafters
Only something grey with a heart
no bigger than a slug, could survive here

        Hiding out in the stairwell with my radio
        waiting for Donovan — *Hurdy Gurdy Man*
        Sunshine Superman

Last scene:

                         Be careful:
Dragged off the street
       into a holding tank   Any show of emotion
                     and they come after you

Second Take: with syringes

Express less anger, resistance   Tie you down
                             Stab you in the ass
                        Express less
                          anger, resistance

     Third Take:
Slumped in the corner   I'm subdued by the threat of *Look*
dazed into the camera   *Electric Shock Treatments*

I tell myself none of this is real..
                  I tell myself this isn't happening....

6 am:
stripped free of the silver lamé
halter top, black tights
I have the signed voucher -
my release slip
paid well for a fraud...

                 Possibly incurable, they say
                 I'll n ever get out of here
                 They want my assets turned over
                 to the federal government —
                 a ward of the state
                 (........................X...........................)

The sound of cars on the boulevard
The comfort of my own coat
A bruised sky softening
from blue to lilac

Released against doctors' orders
Glorious summer!
paranoid schizophrenia
buried in the garden
The familiar dog at my side
I slip off the choke chain
imagine us   happy

The Golden State

Where does it start
this terror?
Returning to L.A.
years later
the air crackling with voices

On Sunset Blvd.
unable to breathe
your legs fail

Remembering the fumes of Kyphi
carrying you away
Pandora's Kitchen
behind the dark curtain
a taste of the exotic

Because you knew the password —
names of living gods
doors that should never open
did

Easy to escape a person, continent
but a Covenant is tenant forever

No truancy in the sun's steady gaze
The Santa Anas blow crazy
on the meridian
Their sirens make a desert of the soul

The hills blaze above the San Fernando
The guns back from Vietnam
have found new enemies

Although you recovered the land of snow -
a poultice of ice on the temple, wrist and neck
the cold wasn't enough to keep you

awake and alive
With the music of complicity
thundering in the head -
Calif, Caliph, calf
fornia, fornication
The golden state, golden calf
The power of seduction
seduction of power

When you fall on your knees
it is without an altar before you
or ground beneath you
the air shut out

Knowing it is *Nothing*
that brought you down -
a vacuum of chaos and emptiness
swarming, thriving

And like a tablet of stone
this judgement breaks
into consciousness
its knowledge - deliverance
or death

Gone to the Dogs

Once you had cottontails
dreaming under tropical palms
doves cooing in the pantry
green lizards eating out of your hand

In times of peace and prosperity
the dogs come sniffing around
bearing gifts of luck and magic -
white feather and rabbits foot
You don't realize what you have
is already taken

They install themselves
at the foot of your life
in postures of servitude
fetch and heel
at your command

Lean against your thigh
heads nuzzled in your lap
furry bellies and muscled flanks
beg to be touched

In the heat of their panting
you are down on all fours
with their long red tongues
rooting for the smell of sweet decay
that clings to their coats

Amazing stamina
as they rise from pools and ditches
renewed by each fresh kill
How you long for those illicit morsels
plundered from the night

Profound vigilance:
Ears perk to the slightest sound
a voice's modulations
Thoughts escape on a breath
audible only to them
The body's braille, its sharp scent of fear
The air electric with encroaching danger

Their padded feet alert you to nothing
It's already too late by the time you see
the torn sheet and marked corners
their hackles raised, teeth gleaming

In dreams, your key no longer fits
and all your weight's pressed against the door
a wolf's snout wedged between you and safety

Or unable to cry out or resist
a seeing-eye dog nudges you on
and you can't tell how close you are
to the cellar stairs...

When they've lapped up every bit of goodness
they give back what is yours -
the empty store of secrets
the fondled dream

You wake alone
a stranger

INDEPENDENCE DAY

Barefoot on the road
down from the old plantation house
you are struck by silence -
Gates locked, blinds drawn
stillness draped in bougainvillea

Spanish moss hangs from ancient cypress
like the matted locks of the Nazarite
like something from a lost world -
Isadora's scarf
the seaweed of Ophelia's hair

Just enough wind to make voices
out of shadows
Not that you expect a posse
this close to beach resorts
this far from Trench Town

Once in sight of the green bay
vendors should be calling out
children ready with a stream of urine -
a salve for tourists stung by sea urchins

In the open air cafe
only dancers from the topless bar
their eyes harder than bullets

At the bottom of the hill
a clot of darkness:
man with the devil's hand -
fingernails curved and black
claws of a carrion bird

Stones turn to gall
The gutted path
doubles you over

A woman in Sunday best
white hat and dress
scoops you into a taxi
Her patois resonant with scripture
expels the *blackheart*
scavenger of souls

No sound of celebration
this Jamaica Independence Day
just a new slant
on the meaning of freedom

In Your Wake

Our parents never knew about the cliffs
how we scrambled up the side like lizards
and jumped forty feet into black water
Javelins thrown to the wind
we trusted our lean bodies to clean flight
Thirty years ago
       before gravity
            and the elements began
                  to work against us
before we stumbled on doubt -
    stones turned
          on weighted steps

Why are we back here
stranded in a tin boat
our watches and rings
grown heavy as lead sinkers
all eyes anchored on you
scoring that steep slope alone

Noticing for the first time
how smooth and treacherous
granite snakes through ridges
how easily shale slivers and fossils scab
the tentative moss clinging to wet slabs

we hardly see your body
bounce off those crags

See only the sun shatter
diamonds on the surface

in your wake
a sliding glass door
close behind you

ATONEMENT

Atonement day comes early
Leaves rust in the exhausted season
I am a part of what the wind pushes away
The dam remains, a barrier
where paint dries under an old sun
Dangerous Undertow
No Swimming, Boating

I don't look down
on the heart of the deluge
where we stood in full summer
backs to the wall
soul and marrow joined
on the narrow ledge under the falls

Gasping from that spray of pure oxygen
this is what you thought God should be
a deafening roar, a floodgate opening
something more solid than light
beauty, fury bearing down on you

An instant leap out of our skins
plunged again, again into the magnetic
current, the spirit
      left us downriver
             hearts pounding
                   between black rocks
on a shore lined with hemlock and pine
a new sky looking over us

This is where you stood
on a day like no other
Life melted into one
      absolute moment
Even the clouds fell for you
thunderstruck
water   crowned
wrapped you in a flood of power
God's coming

The Basket

    i

They hung Eljaro in a basket

to melt his clay feet
to raise the forces
spilling out from his extremities

The land sailor turned
a shade of artichoke
soft at the core and bitter

The dogs fell upon his clothes
but soon lost interest
The vultures circled
but did not descend

His wife, trimming back the prickly pear
hummed a different tune
Everyone scratched him from their ledgers
Even death, stalking him for the last time
settled quietly in his closet like an old shoe

Though night would not restore his dreams
or the rain anoint him
the sky held to his forehead like a magnet
and the sun, a third eye, bald and holy
consumed his vision

Many times he wanted to cry out
but remembered his sister
learned to imitate the crows
and hordes of them blackened the roof
The neighbours crossed themselves
and opened fire
By morning her voice was gone

(her husband, the cheap fiestaware)
The crows clicked their tongues like castanets
and flew off
cursing fluently in Spanish

    ii

For two years, Eljaro hung
in an empty interval
uncounted among the living
and the dead
He imagined he distilled
the body of Christ
in a roman candle
in a single thought
and when the lesions of earth
swallowed him up
he funded the power
to roll away the rock

The Voices once carved in stone
rumbled into silence:
(This is your portion in the land of the...living
There is no memory in the...grave)

He left his body on the wall
and passed the sepulchre
of his own private history:
(dead fields, broken hands
rich landowners, a spiteful bride)

And the history of the village:
(built around a visitation
of The Holy Mother weeping -
a fountain shrine, a pig trough
a wading pool, where old men spat
children pissed and virgins
threw their coins)

Eljaro removed the small vial
of Our Lady
from around his neck
and threw her acid tears
on his binding cords

The basket fell

His body freed its last sparks
the petrified egg of his reptilian heart
a flint against the standing stones:
(the governing heads of lost kingdoms
the remnants of his culture -
to each his own stranger)

      iii

Eljaro returned to the desert
to thank his oppressors
but they had vanished

so he set out in search of the weaver of baskets

I Have The Power

It's a matter of alignment you say
as you pass through the wall
not magic but frequency
Brushing the atoms from you like plaster
you slip into me
I believe you
I am a woman
I have the power of opening
You however must cup your hands in prayer
match resonance with the right mantra
with something other than chance
(Flattery is known to help
That's how the Red Sea parted)

No one disappears into thin air
They just live beside us
in other songs

You reach under the hood of my pelvis
like Houdini's last attempt
at something there is no way out of

Shadowcrossing

> *...we recognize our own rejected thoughts;*
> *they come back to us with a sense of alienated majesty*
> —Emerson

I'm caught in the interval
between worlds
like a shortwave radio
a station out of range

The man asleep beside me
who curves around my nights
like a familiar moon
doesn't know
I have almost forgotten him
I will have to tell the children -
those deer lost in the headlights
of the television
I am not quite their mother
our reality is less probable
than that shifting screen

I cross the shadow
on a path chosen to a path disdained
Parallel journeys are taken
This is the crossroads
where destinies intersect -
the darkness before ascension

Nothing is forsaken:
What went on living without me
comes back
like an orphaned child
begging for remembrance

BLOOD OF THE EARTH

The Next Move

Lakeside ceremonies of fire and wine
Back when the world looked after itself
You said we were reserved for something different
Pure magic

Years later, on a smoldering beach
the car off the cliff
will be yours and mine
Amazing, the radio still plays
Stairway to Heaven

Though legs are broken against the dash
between the minefield and the landfill
there's another highway

Do you think we can make it?
Your touch is laminated with sunscreen
and pale promise
We're the thrashing of beached fish
in a moment filled with sand and oil -
the batter of love and greed

Gear up for the next move:
Dead or alive
one drop of blood
a scrap of DNA
and they make fresh copies of us
Real voodoo

What you meant by different?

BATTLE OF THE PINES
for Ellen Gabriel and Denise David

At the beach in Kanehsatake
a statue overlooks the St. Lawrence
overlooks all that has happened
for almost two centuries
Our Lady of Constant Sorrow:
a broken crown, a baby torn from her
hand - the stump of benediction

She stands as a reminder of those
who would not submit to the church
who held to the Longhouse
Denied firewood, whole families
froze to death in the bitter Quebec winter

Tonight we sleep among the pines
in sight of those who planted them
buried nearby
alongside the bunkers -
a barricade of trees
overlooking Oka
The blue shadow
of a man in uniform
floats down the hill
to the valley below

Tomorrow we remember the victory
of life's passage over a golf course
of passion over political will
Tonight we expect helicopters
to circle overhead
Tomorrow, a thanks giving -
music and prayer

The Clan mothers show us
where the SQ opened fire

A year to the day. The trees' wounds
ooze with sap. The children still weep

There are no flowers
at the foot of the statue
where the army crept in at midnight
where the Clan mothers stood their ground
A daughter wears a scar above her breast -
the tip of a bayonet
There will be drums before dawn

Seminole come
lay their hands on the wood
The bark heals over
but the smoke still hangs
where AKs split the air
dividing loyalties
in the heart of a nation

Justice, a blind statue
Truth in the trunk of a tree
Those who walk between them
unreconciled

CROSSOVER

I come back to you
from the caravan
the music of the Islands
sharing the air with a dozen fiery tongues

You can imagine kilted virgins
dancing over crossed swords
and Transylvanians bowing to each other
over house wine
You believe me
when I say there was no talk of blood

But Palestinians setting up shop
with a rainbow of blown glass
and the dowry dolls of refugees
has you wondering
if terrorists carry mother of pearl
crosses and ivory inlaid guitars
across the border

The falafels you know about

In Central America, they're sure
we're all bald
white, ruthless bankers
But you, darker than the cedars
of Lebanon
ain't no pimp in a pink fedora

I show you my name
written in Arabic
looks like the last strands of wheat
in an October field
Isn't it beautiful?

When the world switches on
at 6 pm
there will be rumours of war
on the same fields
we crossed over in song

a whole confederation of rotting fruit
and more empty mouths
stuffed with manure

What Would You Do Anyway?

Forget Paradise
its gates guarded by angels
beautiful and deadly
What would you do there anyway?

Forget the heartpoppy
pinned to your sleeve
its red pout black
at the centre

Silence the debates
lower the flags
As long as there are still women
tricked into brothels
children maimed by war
       we fail

The news reels on
Runes cast against the spirit's
indecipherable math
prove nothing but that we live
within a fraction of chance

Death cells divide and multiply
You've seen the thumbprints
on the eyelids of the newborn

Beyond the reach of love
and scope of magic
It passes all understanding

The same said of faith

Dreamers Rock

    i

At dawn, the island emerges
like the back of an ancient turtle

Camped on white rock, my daughter says
is the skull of a sleeping giant
one breath is a lifetime
the slow centuries moving under us

Belongings discarded among the pines
we lie oblivious to reeling gulls
The sun incubates in stone
A phoenix egg fills the hollows of our backs
We dream blue flame and fruits spring from secret clefts

If we never wore shoes again
like the man in the Andes
who grew small trees from the cracks in his feet
       our bodies strong, earthbaked...
If we stayed here long enough
beside the drumming waves
we would hear the true music of our names
       wed stars to our reflections

    ii

Tourists leave
a trail of waste

In the distance, machines
idle on steel bridges

The trees are marked and dynamite set
There is talk of condominiums

iii

This is the way back
through the debris of shards and mortar
blueberries crushed, still warm in our hands

The firebird
above the power lines
regards us
with scarlet eyes scarcely human

The faultline of their city—
the womb we rise out of

POST WAR

You have outlived the night and its awful secrets
the heart and its need for more blood
Returning from a lost land
with the bronze and chiselled hands
of the war memorial man
nothing changed but the guard
the imperial sun - a discus overthrown

You left the trenches for a cigarette
a pension, swapped sniper vision
for a clear shot of brandy

Peace is a profound loneliness
(nothing worn lightly -
a bolt of silk, a ripple of love)
Trust is her companion
nestled in your shoulder
like a sleeping gun
You awaken to a ghost wind
and a vanishing

The dream is always the same:
You watch the honeysuckle
climb through an open window
entwine you in tenderness or terror
moments before the atom splits
the world into scattered particles...
Except for the silence (especially of birds)
everything seems utterly alive -
The chair, a dance of molecules
your cup - a lake of fire

You hardly remember the other signs
    cactus dropping their spines
        fish leaping the banks
            mountains trembling

      wombs unable
        to bear
         fruit

Is this the final war
the numbers stacked against us
like a deck of cards?

There are no fortunes to be told
We're living in the future
and the future is old

The Moon Had A Sister

There is a good chance, according to a new paper appearing in the journal 'Nature', that the moon we know so well once had a sister.
— Time Magazine, October 6, 1997

They would not call it birth
but *cosmic crackup*
(the feminine, always associated
with things unstable, unpredictable)
disintegration, dark and lunar

It is true
our love was a head-on collision
the size of mars
and short-lived as any hot pursuit
I, Mother Earth
was taken by force
and the labour difficult
My satellites had to be carved out
like raw giblets
So much debris hurled into space -
The sky, a wet nurse

What stirred at my core
as light, aura of another
a saturnesque ring of rubble
formed into a sphere
separating, to create
an inner and outer moon -
(alas, one dead
within a hundred years)
the magnet of love
the grip of gravity
not enough to hold them both:
the *inner* drawn back to me
so violently, she disappeared
Or so they say
(in their finite wisdom)

The soul will not be born
in time or space
but lies behind
all that is manifest

I, Mother Earth
will always have one moon
tugging at my tidal waters
content, that inner twin
untouched by outer worlds
is able to sustain her sister
even in death

BLACKTHORN WINTER

We're down
to the skeletons of trees
bare bones of winter
The wind thieves
the heart's flickering heat

With less sense than rabbits
in their invisible mounds
the bear in muzzled sleep
we brave this cold season
dream down the sun
leap years, live
in those lost hours

Confound the bitter queen
whose fingers are the stubs
of stars and splintered moon
her mirror glare of ice
the slippery path
where the strong and fair have fallen

What The Thunder Brings

The day the sky rolls with thunder
and the north wind dashes the waves to shore
when the oil drums under the floating dock
scrape and grind against the rocks
we hogtie the boat to rubber bumpers
the canoe is airborne
and the maples double over in spasms

Father stands on the brink
with his block and tackle
his voice beating down on us -
A flash of sheet lightning
The sting of driving rain

Later, such heat
lawn chairs blister, grass singes
Father leaves off shouting
takes us to town
where we are put to wait
between the liquor store and garage
While he fills the tank
and the trunk with Seagrams
a car's towed in
front end pulverized
windshield smeared with blood
The door swings open
One spike heeled shoe spills out
white and dainty
the kind Marilyn Monroe wore
when her dress flew up
We can't help looking
as if there should be something more -
a show of flesh
to throttle the imagination

'Drunks,' father tells us
as if accidents don't happen
to good people
His 'don't stare' ushers us away -
the same disgusted tone
reserved for Mongoloids
spotted in the supermarket
strapped to wheelchairs
or winos in the street
baring wooden teeth
the raised, crooked fingers
that hook in the eye:
Spectacles of human waste
Disasters to turn from

Even in Montreal
at the House of Midgets
where we paid good money to see
he orders us to go blind
Like in a circus mirror
unable to confront
the twisted shape of our own thoughts
the ticket stubs burn in clenched fists

When we return
the waves have licked the rocks clean
and the wind's blown the heads off
mom's geraniums
My sister and I put on swimsuits
Father's voice is carried away
by scolding chipmunks
and unnoticed, under the turquoise dock
spiders clinging to rusty oil drums
are fighting for their lives

Accidents

Outside in the blizzard
it's bumper to bumper
For the moment we're safe
We survived the stirfry
at the *Light Waves Cafe*
Sprouts like giant sperm
expire on our plates
but you won't be satisfied
until the soul rises
on the steam of our cappuccino

There are no accidents, you say
We are bound by unspoken agreements
the ordinance of fate
and by a god's unfailing hand
neatly filed
like incoming/outgoing mail

I go along for the ride
tell you about a red convertible
at the height of summer
the beautiful young men I made love to
on smoking wheels and scorched upholstery
our hair pinned to the wind
How on a whim I jumped out
for wilder flowers blooming in the ditch -
something to place on their bodies
after they were hauled down the hill
one by one
into the arms of mothers
who went mad
with grief and guilt and longing
    golden rod, purple flocks
      courageous among the burrs and thistles

It's what you want to hear
isn't it?

Or how Karen
anxious to tell the story of Gerda Taro
crushed under a tank in the Spanish Civil War
gathers the documents, mounts her bike
and falls under the wheels of a truck
at Bloor and Church
      Only minutes before
leaving her last words at my door:
I feel I'm really close

I tell you
I have seen that car come
time and time again
whenever life reaches its exquisite limit -
a climax that is the magnet
of death and desire

And though I pray, I don't believe
my life so precious
Even those in the midst of great missions
have died badly

I tell you
we are none of us above
bribing the ferryman
outsmarting the killer
applauding the brilliant
narrow escape

In the service of nothing but fear
I work against time
and save what I can
from the clutches of darkness

Whether or not we choose

from a fixed menu
isn't the point
it's that sooner or later
the cup comes up empty

Tonight, we'll walk
or hail a cab
For you, in your infinite trust
whatever happens
it will be as it should

The Lake Thereafter
for Larry

You'll ride out in the red canoe
I have left you
the mist steaming off the lake
each paddle stroke a year
till you arrive at the distance
we have travelled together
You won't drop anchor
but let the wind work
its miracle of motion
as it has always done

You'll think: Some resting place this
lake drags docks and concrete blocks
miles from their moorings

As if I would agree to settle
in the earth like a shrub
with a slab that needed tending
I want to be light as the leaves
that drift to your feet
a snowflake melting in your hair

Would you have it any other way
my champion racer
but to dance on the rudder of chance
merge with wind and water?

The star shooting from the heavens
leaves a trail of blue smoke
You know what it's like
when the checkered flag falls -
the waters of space churning
the heart pure lava, your body
released like a bow...

Remember me
flying barefoot over the stones
wanting nothing more
than to dive deep into the lake's arms

Centre your sites on the horizon
Let the memory of sand sift through your hands
and spread me out like an altar cloth
over this magnificent table of water

The Ghost of God
A Requiem in Earth Minor

You're just a shell, a feather
I found on the beach and left behind

Once you roamed the forest
entering animals and dreams
Now we keep you in this storage room
with xmas decorations
and indestructible plastics

Over feast and funeral
you preside like an old debt returning
Your stare is like a blank cheque
and I don't know what I'm supposed to pay

You tremble at the centre of my heart
but you don't speak your mind
and the heart's like a grenade
detonated when we run out of time

You must live in a blue-veined field
where the clouds mute your footsteps
I can't hear above the moans
of a world that you left in decline

Set apart like all good prisoners
too pure for the world
you wait in a vacuum
perfecting punishments
releasing the 20th century malaise:
We will pay for greasing Ezekiel's wheel

I've forgotten your dimensions
that the wind was once your scarf
on a breath that rose and fell
like an empire of lost possibilities

I require only food, sleep, shelter
respite from the probing darkness
but you require nothing
Though I offered myself up with wine and flares
I could not bow to you in your great heights

*You ride over my memory
with your boots on every track
like the ghost of a lover
but there's no turning back*
to forever

Much later in the spent light
a terrified child
full of amends and apologies
knocks at your door:
*Can you compete with neon and 24 hrs of free
entertainment?
Try.*

The books say you want my heart
but what is a heart?
A pump organ without strings
a fist without wings
an orb, fearful of extinction

The same song plays over and over
Crazy, crazy, crazy for you

Who holds the key?
(Why have you forsaken me?)
Who holds the key?
(Why have you forsaken me?)

The Book Of Weeds

*A plant leans towards the light
but its seeds germinate in darkness*

IDENTIFICATION

Weeds, the Devil's salad
grow rapidly and thrive
without cultivation

Herbacious and cunning
undaunted by unfavorable conditions
they leech goodness from the earth
choking out all that lies in their path

Should lamb's quarters appear in the garden
expect the slaughter of innocent children

Goutweed and *liverwort* portend illness in the home
Spotted spurge - an epidemic
Spatterdock - no hope for recovery

Creeping charlie indicates robbery
quack grass or *foxtail* -
treacherous colleagues

Ever baneful
bindweed denotes witchcraft
stinking hellebore, a menial vocation
henbit, a demanding wife

Left unchecked they multiply like triffids
entering through window cracks, holes of doubt
chinks in the armour of pride:
Horehound attacks the weak joints of lust
as do *smut rye* and *swamp beggar* tick

PRECAUTIONS

Remove *staghorn* from the rose bed
Tend to seeds of statice, *Queen Anne's lace*...
Trim dead wood from *Jacob's ladder*

Wave a willow switch
should you encounter a *wing nut*
or *wild nard* in the forest

Avoid treading on *viper's bugloss*
Recite the 23rd psalm
within a hectare of *hoary pucoon*

PREPARATIONS

Against stinging nettle apply *balm of Gilead*
For eruptions of yellow toad flax —
a tincture of *Job's tears*
If stricken with *tuberous vetching*
inhale the vapours of *baby's breath*

In extremity don a shield of *blessed thistle*

CONTROL

One must first invite the host
the minions of mealy bugs -
wireworms and blistermites
midges and slugs

Lay siege on the equinox moon
Leave a dish of beer
near the mouth of a lily
Encircle with sage and marigold

Bonsai!
Collect vermin on virgin parchment
Transfer to the offending weeds

To insure blight and dieback
one must invoke
the vile anatomy of Beelzebug:
>   *Clubroot and collar rot*
>   *take a firm hold*
>   *Crown gall, blackleg*
>   *fungus and mould!*

>   *Scab and scale*
>   *scrub the hill bald*
>   *canker, chafers*
>   *chanking and scald!*

Cover flowers and vegetables
all fruit bearing trees
in *monk's hood* and *maidenhair*
Place *Solomon's Seal* at four corners
Annoint with oil of *angelica*

Root out evil
Starve the Fiend
Pray for plenty
in the harvest of pure souls

TRUE COLOURS

Rota

Tarot, the lexigram for Tora/Rota, is a pictorial view of the astrological wheel and the Tree of Life, codified to protect practitioners from ecclesiastical henchmen.
  —Ruminations for Bryan Dobbs

You are unconcerned
as to how many angels
I have balanced on my turntable
We already agree on everything

But you know this orchard better than I -
the fig and the pomegranate
the first flag, the fatal kiss
all the telling signs

There are a few facts I've missed
(cool metatrons I cannot touch)
Tell me again
it was an ant and not a mountain
that brought the giant down
The small things undo us
The things we have undone

A child shall lead us
into the Greater Arcana

Do not despair
if I should sing
with a sword and a cup
about the face
that launched a thousand missiles
whose silhouette
I still fall prey to

Because you welcomed the old gods
into this house of cards
the sun shines with two eyes and a mouth

once more
There are no romans
with crossed staves in your deck -
a hood for death to hide behind
You have cut the hanged man free

I see the play of events
stripped of irony
The distance between two things disappears
in vibrant synchronicity

The blank rune
could be a pillar of salt
or full moon
It may be upright or inverted
like a mutable star

I don't know

the unuttered Word
the unaltered Space
this wheel was made for

These things have been given
for you to understand

THE COLOURS OF LOVE
for Chela Rhea

Though half and half makes whole
my fair-haired one asks
which part of her is white
which black

Daughter, the Sahara
drifted to my doorstep
and you were sifted
from my body, tough
and golden as wet sand

Your Baltic blue eyes
a tributary: Indian Ocean
crossed Tropic of Capricorn
to join the North Sea
(In the chalice of the heart
our blood mixed like wine)

When niece and nephew
tumble out, flushed as apples
fresh hybrids flesh out the family tree

Minced words, the world pared down
to softer sounds - Mulatto...Metis...
all of us native somewhere
(indigenous and deposed)
watch the same sun rise
and fall, expel old airs

Let me hold you here
daughter, nephew, niece
in the full circle of my arms
Your upturned faces -
half moon, half rainbow

True Colours

I always dream of fish
when I conceive
Great, golden fish
shaped like Greecian urns

The night before labour
I fly low over freshly tilled fields
dressed in mother of pearl
and abalone

When drawn to a man
I dream wild horses
venture into far fields
for the touch of a tossled mane
Oh the way their flesh ripples down to the flank
that dark, delicious smell of them
how they never take their eyes off you

Sometimes birds appear -
those brilliant, fleeting messengers...
The day an *Indigo Bunting* visited my feeder
then vanished like a flash of neon blue light -
a bird rarely seen north of Virginia -
the long distance call came
to say you had survived
against all odds

These are the true colours
of grace and gratitude

Butterfly Picking

They ricochet off car windshields
or pinned to the grill
whistle like crepe paper
hung for a wedding
It's a miracle
some still have wings
their velvet bodies
black stems without them

Walking along the shoulder of the road
we bend and pick butterflies
Those still twitching we'll try to keep
alive all summer
flightless on the screened porch
in a basket of grass
on a diet of milkweed and daisies
a thimble of water
My daughter tells me
the painted lady prefers zinnia
the viceroy - aster

We fill a margarine container
with admiral and buckeye
monarch and mourning cloak
a flush of tropical brilliance
Inhabitants of a finer world
displaced on this dense and hulking highway
they belong on the lips of trumpet lilies
in the ruffles of peonies and roses
to rise like parasols
over the heads of the fairies
my daughter still believes in

Like kisses blown from the hand
or wishes that fly

weightless into the current of dreams
she will redeem them
and when the cold days come
mount under glass
in monuments of driftwood
the myth of immortality

Day of the First Mother

You take what is left
of the iris, lupin, columbine -
all that is purple
On this day you will walk
with a royal colour

The old woman watches you
from her window
your arms filled with flowers
How easily the heads droop -
shock of being torn from the root

You are the cutting she raised
from unknown stock
only the columbine native to this soil
the rest, hybrids - delicate, unsure

You glance back at the pond
on your way to the car
the children, thankfully with you
a mallard followed by ducklings

The driveway slopes downward with stones
The old woman, still in her dressing gown
descends slowly, steps in the shadow of a hawk
fleeing from a small bird -
the anger of an empty nest

There is no time to mourn
You are on your way
to meet the stranger who gave you life
The old woman hands you a vase
Tell her...a gift
a daughter for a pitcher of water

When you meet the first mother
lock eyes, embrace
the eternity of lost years
your arms release flowers
she, the fragrance of *white diamonds*

Coming back to the garden
with a book of love poems she gives
you find this:

With you here at Mertu
is like being at Heliopolis already

We return to the tree-filled garden
my arms filled with flowers

Looking at my reflection in the still pool -
my arms filled with flowers -
I see you creeping on tip-toe
to kiss me from behind
my hair heavy with perfume

With your arms around me
I feel as if I belong to the Pharaoh *

   * Anonymous Egyptian poet (1567 - 1085 B.C.)
     Poems of Love, A Treasury of Verse, Running Press, PA.

The Call

*And he will give his angels charge over thee
lest thou dash thy foot against a stone*

Half a lifetime later
the call comes
marking his existence

your humble beginnings left
for strangers to disclose

*The Father has chosen
to remain anonymous*
but the gloved hand sheds
a thread of evidence

How after your birth
a world away
he and siblings flourished
young champions in Olympic Games

You want him to know you
won trophies too
falling just short of the torch
he brought home proud

You want him to know you
sang loud and long
such yearning
that bells rang out in public places
      in the small chance
he might have heard

You want him to know you
are the prize he never claimed

Eye, sinew, bone
created in his image
a body wired for sound
wound for flight

frightened by inertia, silence

How can the search be over, race done?

You want to be remembered by him
thrust back to that place
preserved by memory -
a ghost with the power to haunt

Instead, as a mother
fierce for your own flesh and blood
you linger, tuck daughters in
a room without shadows
whisper *I love you*
don't ever forget how much

A Far Cry

It takes two days
Nemaska, then Chisasibi
Almost at the treeline
the landscape dwindles
to jack pine
Towns evaporate

No roads before the dams -
surging waters gagged and harnessed
Now stopped rapids -
boulders black and menacing
like a pile up of cars
and where 10,000 caribou drowned -
the methane of rotting vegetation
Miles of scrub and sky
a cold desert highway -
chinks in the Canadian Shield

At check point
the drummer taps his knees
The story of *Malcolm* slips off his lap
Son of a diplomat
a solitary black boy in Ottawa
his thoughts are impossible to read

We're unlikely tourists
They want I.D.
In history class I learned
my people were savages
The bass player nods. He's Cree

It's all a front the glossy brochures
They're tracking threats to the infrastructure -
the next White Whale Project

The land quakes under the weight
of man-made rivers
White fish, mercury-tainted
glow in the dark
Those who eat them feel the tremors

Startled by huskies with ice-blue eyes
at rest stops he sticks with Malcolm
his own canteen and dwindling supplies
In Pretoria I walked on the hoods of cars
to escape the dogs

Night falls under the grit of stars
a cloud of gravel
We are like a lost migration of geese
over James Bay
Most of us died on merchant ships
packed together like sardines

Malcolm slips off the map
X marks the spot, a thousand miles
from nowhere

At journey's end
there are cook tents waiting -
bannock, berries and moose
a bonfire, honour drum
fiddles, step dancing

First black they've seen
except on T.V.
Children touch his wooly hair
He is something wild and rare
like the random appearance
of a wolf or bear
He has never been made to feel
this welcome

It's a far cry from Africa
further still from the Capital —
this part of Canada
he never knew existed

The Lake in July

This is the day you longed for
months ago
under a blanket of snow
To close your eyes
and see the sun
streaked in waves under your lids
the shadow of your lover
crossing over
a bridge into new lands:
berries filled with blood
cedar thick with musk
his taste on your tongue

Doors flung open
your sheets set sail on twin maples
The body sheds its dying cells
for stars stolen from the night

You open your eyes
to the mauve lake
a shroud at daybreak:
the outline of the trees
the outline of your life
liquid, shimmering
like a song sent out over water

You wonder how long
the earth has been soiled
the heart this heavy

The lake accepts your tears
To her you are weightless
What isn't swallowed up
is drifting away
drowning or being born
Apart from the wind
ruffling the surface

what else actually happens?

ABOUT THE AUTHOR

Lea Harper is a poet and songwriter living near Omemee, Ontario where she teaches guitar and writes. As a musician and singer, she has performed in Los Angeles, Jamaica and South America. Her group Syren was nominated for a Juno and won the Canadian Reggae Award for Best Duo. Her songs are currently receiving airplay in Taiwan and South Africa. All That Saves Us, published by Black Moss Press, was her first collection of poems.

Harper has received awards for her poetry as well, including The LaPointe Prize, the Icarus competition and The People's Political Poem contest.